SPECIAL SAINTS ❧ FOR ❧ SPECIAL PEOPLE

Stories of Saints with Disabilities

MEGAN C. GANNON

FOREWORD BY MAUREEN PRATT, *author of Salt and Light: Church, Disability, and the Blessing of Welcome for All*

TWENTY-THIRD PUBLICATIONS
twentythirdpublications.com

Many thanks to my family and friends
who encouraged me not to give up on this project.
Writing a book was the last thing I thought
I would ever do, and there were many times
I thought it was a crazy idea and that I should drop it.
However, each time I got up the nerve to share it with you,
your positive words kept me going.
God bless you all.

TWENTY-THIRD PUBLICATIONS
One Montauk Avenue, Suite 200 • New London, CT 06320
(860) 437-3012 or (800) 321-0411 • www.twentythirdpublications.com

Illustrations by Lila M. Carnevale. Permission for use was granted by the Lila
M. Carnevale Estate and the Nicholas and Lila Carnevale Living Trust.

ISBN: 978-1-62785-484-9 • Printed in the U.S.A.

 A division of Bayard, Inc.

CONTENTS

MEGAN GANNON *has worked as webmaster for many small businesses, organizations, and parishes. In 2014, she took a part-time position as a software engineer with a contractor for NASA's Goddard Space Flight Center. Born with cerebral palsy, Megan has persevered through many physical obstacles, including speech impairment and quadriplegia.*

LILA CARNEVALE *was a retired personnel analyst for the Fairfax County Government in Virginia. She was so inspired by reading **Special Saints for Special People** that, at age 83, she returned to her love of sketching, drawing all of the saints included in this book. She had been fighting breast cancer since 2002. She also suffered congestive heart failure in 2013 but continued to have a lively spirit until her death in July 2015.*

FOREWORD

When I was a child and very ill (many times!), I pored through the pages of a book on the saints. The lives I read about were very interesting and spiritually formational. But, among the many examples included in the rather thick book, none seemed very easy to relate to for me, a young Catholic with serious health problems.

Today, children (and adults) with disabilities are blessed to have Megan Gannon's *Special Saints for Special People*, a gem of a book that helps all of us, young or older, understand that persons with disabilities have been and are today called to service, holiness, and sainthood. Among these pages are inspiring, relatable examples of men and women who embraced their lives with personal challenges and answered God's call to service. And, just as inspiring is the insight provided by the author herself, who is no stranger to disability, and who has also answered God's call, recognizing a need for such a volume and filling it wonderfully.

No matter our life challenges and no matter the calling God has given us, *Special Saints for Special People* is an encouraging companion as we, too, strive to bring our unique talents and gifts forward, in loving service to our awesome Creator!

MAUREEN PRATT, author of *Salt and Light: Church, Disability, and the Blessing of Welcome for All*

INTRODUCTION

As a child I never had any special devotions to saints. Mass and the Rosary were part of our family routine, but I don't have any memory of praying to individual saints. This never bothered me or really even crossed my mind. I knew saints were in heaven watching over us and praying for us, but I couldn't really identify with them.

I was born with cerebral palsy. As a child I was just busy trying to be a "normal" kid, going to school, dictating my homework to my mother since I am unable to write, playing with my friends, and taking family vacations.

When I got older and had to choose a saint for my confirmation name, I started with names I liked and then read a little about the saints with those names. I didn't have a clue that there were saints who lived their whole lives with disabilities. And it never occurred to me to try to research that. I did read that St. Teresa of Avila was disabled early in life and was cured through the intercession of St. Joseph, which I thought was cool. A priest happened to give a homily on her the day before I had to make my final decision, so I took that as a sign and chose her for my patron saint. I can't say I would have definitely chosen a saint with a disability even if I knew that was a possibility. Again, I was intent on trying to live like every other young person. On the other hand, I know I would have always turned to these saints in situations that only another disabled person would understand.

As I grew older, I learned of many other saints—like St. André Bessette and St. Padre Pio—who are known for healing others, and I began to realize some were credited with improving the lives of people who had a disability. St. Francis de Sales, for example, invented a sign language so he could communicate and pass on the faith to a deaf man he knew.

I still was completely unaware of saints who themselves were disabled. This is sort of funny to me, since throughout my whole life random people who didn't even know me would call me a saint. They could only see this girl in a wheelchair, unable to speak clearly, and totally dependent on others for almost everything. When I was very young, I hated to be looked at this way because I didn't think of myself as that different from anyone else. As I grew older, it didn't bother me as much, but I wondered why they would say I was a saint. After all, it was my family, friends, teachers, and therapists who did everything for me and allowed me many of the same experiences that other children and young adults enjoyed. I am totally dependent on others for everything. I don't have very good control of my muscles, so I need help with things like eating, getting dressed, and taking a shower. My speech is also very hard to understand unless you are around me for a while, so I usually need a friend or family member to tell others what I'm saying. It is only with the aid of a very special computer that I am able to type by just using my eyes, since I don't have enough control over my hands to use a keyboard or mouse.

When I was in college, I had a good friend who had a relative with an intellectual disability. She asked me if I knew of any saints that her relative might be interested in knowing more about. We flipped through some saint books I had on a shelf but once again came up empty. I basically concluded there weren't any. It's not like people with disabilities are usually known for feeding the hungry, taking care of the sick, or spreading the Good News. More often than not, we are usually on the receiving end of others' works of mercy.

Only recently through the internet have I discovered there are many saints who were born with or who had disabilities most of their lives. For as long as I can remember, I have loved the saying that some attribute to Saint Mother Teresa, "What you are is God's gift to you. What you make of yourself is your gift to God." Most people accept their disabilities. Sure, there are times when we wish we weren't disabled, and sure, we do often hope for a miracle, but if we stop to think about it, everyone wants to change something about themselves.

In this book, I have chosen to focus on some holy persons who accepted themselves and never received a miraculous cure. Some of these special saints may be known to you already. You may also meet some new saints. I have included a few that still are awaiting the approval of a second miracle before officially being recognized as a saint by the church. They are called blessed, and maybe they will be declared a saint by helping you.

Reading stories about saints is meant to inspire and encourage us. I hope these special saints do this for you. Enjoy!

SPECIAL SAINTS FOR SPECIAL PEOPLE

BLESSED MARGARET OF CASTELLO

Patron of People Who Are Blind,
Deformed, Hunchbacked,
or Unwanted

LONG TIME AGO, IN 1287, THERE LIVED A BRAVE NOBLEMAN AND HIS WIFE. They lived in a castle called Metola, which is southeast of what is now Florence, Italy. They were very excited, because they were expecting a baby. They were hoping for a son to follow in his father's footsteps and become the next great military leader of their country, which is now part of Italy. They wanted all the people to share in their happiness when the baby was born, so they planned a great feast with many celebrations for everyone. The whole country was waiting to hear the good news. Bells were to be rung, everyone would stop working, and parties and festivals would start everywhere for people of all ages to enjoy.

The big day finally came, but there were no bells and no celebrations, and the feast was canceled. No one knew what was happening. In time they came to believe that the baby didn't live, and everyone was sad and disappointed. But sometimes what people think isn't what is actually true.

In fact, the noble lady did have her baby, but it was not at all what they were expecting. First, the baby was a girl, not a boy. That was a great disappointment, since a girl at that time couldn't become a military leader. But it was a lot more than that.

This baby was very different from most babies. One of her legs was much shorter than the other. Her face didn't look "pretty" as other babies' faces do. They soon realized she was blind. She was smaller than other children, and she had a hunchback, so she would never be able to stand up straight.

Because of all her problems, her parents were too embarrassed and ashamed to let anyone know she was their daughter. They didn't even want anyone to know she was alive. They didn't consider her to be part of the family and wouldn't even give her a name. A servant took the baby to the church to be baptized and named her Margaret, which means "Beautiful Pearl." This was an odd name to give her, since nobody thought she was very pretty at all.

Little Margaret was hidden in the castle, and only a few servants who took care of her knew she even existed. One day, when Margaret was about six, she was making her way around the castle as she liked to do—hobbling along with her bad limp and feeling her way holding on to the walls, since she couldn't see. Someone who was visiting her mother saw her and started talking to her, but a servant rushed in just as the stranger was about to ask Margaret who she was. Her parents' secret was still safe.

Her parents didn't want to take a chance that anything else like that would ever happen again, so her father had a special room added to a small church in the forest, where he made Margaret live all alone. The room didn't have a door. Little Margaret was put inside, and then the last wall was added to lock her in. It only had a window where people could pass food and other things to her. She could also listen to Mass through the window. She stayed in that tiny room for almost thirteen years. By listening to the birds outside she could learn whether spring and summer were coming, which would make her room very hot, or if it was winter, which would explain why she was so cold.

The priest became her good friend and taught Margaret all about God, especially the Holy Family, and how to pray. She also learned she wasn't really alone. Jesus was right there in the tabernacle and she could talk to him whenever she wanted. So that was what she did. She spent all of her time talking and praying to Jesus.

A war broke out in her country, and everyone had to leave. Her father fought in the war. Her family took Margaret to a safer city and hid her in an underground cave. Margaret spent all of her time praying that the war would end quickly and that her father would be safe. She loved her parents very much, even though they never showed her any love. Although Margaret was used to being hidden away all alone, she missed the fresh air and the sounds of the animals and birds. She also really missed listening to Mass and talking to the priest. She had to endure this for over a year.

When the war was over, her parents knew they had to do something with Margaret. They had heard people talking about a church where miracles were happening, and they wanted God to cure Margaret. They knew how much Margaret loved God and thought surely God would answer her prayers. So they took Margaret to this shrine in the town of Castello and ordered her to stay there all day and pray that God would cure her of all that they thought was wrong with her. They didn't even stay with her to pray. Margaret believed that God made her special and God loved her exactly the way she was. She didn't want to disobey her parents, though, so she prayed and asked God to only cure her if he wanted to, but not if he wanted her to stay the way he made her. When her parents returned in the evening, they found her exactly the same. She didn't receive the miracle they were hoping for. They were not happy. So without Margaret knowing it, and without even saying goodbye, they returned home and left Margaret all alone in this strange place.

When night came, the church had to be locked up. Margaret waited on the steps in front of the church, hoping her parents were just late. She stayed there all night. By morning, she realized they weren't coming back for her. She was scared. She was alone, with no money, no extra clothes, and no one to lead her through the streets and crowds. She didn't know what to do. She realized it was time for her to learn to be independent and take care of herself.

Some beggars found her in the morning and were nice to her, and they became her friends. They taught Margaret how to beg for alms to get money on which to live, and they helped her to learn her way around this strange new city. She relied on her cane to guide her and also used it as a crutch to lean on as she limped through the streets. Her new friends helped her find places to sleep at night. Sometimes a farmer would let her stay in his barn, which

Margaret liked a lot because it reminded her of the baby Jesus in Bethlehem. Margaret shared with her friends everything she knew about her faith, especially St. Joseph, who was her favorite saint. She could talk about him for hours. Thanks to Margaret, her new friends began to love God too. They could see what a happy young lady Margaret was, even though almost everything about her life should have upset her.

Eventually, the Dominican sisters saw how holy Margaret was and offered to let Margaret come live with them. They also thought they could help take care of her, but to their surprise, Margaret was quite independent and was more interested in helping others than being helped herself. Margaret was so happy, because not only would she finally have a place to live, but she could also continue to learn about God. She was glad to be part of this new "family" of Dominicans and did everything she could to follow all the rules of the convent.

Some of the sisters, however, didn't take the rules as seriously as Margaret did, and they became jealous that Margaret was living better than they were and doing more to please God. They thought she was showing off. They forced Margaret to decide between easing up on her prayers and good works or leaving them and moving out. This was a very hard decision, and she was confused. She wanted to do what she believed God wanted, but she loved having a place to live and people to call her family. In the end, Margaret knew she had to do what she thought would please God. She would depend on God to take care of her, so she left the convent.

All of her poor friends welcomed her back. Some families would try to let Margaret stay in their homes whenever possible. In return, Margaret would do whatever she could to help them. She would babysit so the parents could work to earn money. She would help the children with their homework, which is amazing since Margaret never had an education. It was a special grace from God that she knew things on subjects that only educated people usually knew.

During this time, Margaret was invited to join another group of women called the Mantellate, who dedicated themselves to prayer and good works without becoming nuns. She spent her days visiting the sick and people in prison, bringing them food and medicine, and helping them in any way she could. Of course, she also prayed for them all of the time. She was so close to God that often people she prayed for immediately got better. Sometimes she would be in such deep prayer that people said she would be lifted right off the ground. Many people grew closer to God just by watching her example.

After a while, a wealthy family offered to let Margaret come live with them. Margaret agreed but decided to make a little room for herself in the small, cold attic and not in a nice, warm, fancy room where the family wanted her to stay. She spent many hours every day in her room praying. One day a fire broke out and everyone had to get out of the house as fast as possible. They almost forgot about Margaret who, as usual, was in the attic praying. When someone hurried back in to get her, Margaret calmly came downstairs and threw her cloak on the fire, and the fire in the whole mansion immediately went out.

When Margaret was thirty-three, her friends could see that she was getting weak. They knew her body was not as strong as other people's and that their friend would not live much longer. She died on April 13, 1320. That is now her feast day. They truly believed their Margaret was a great saint. After her funeral the priests wanted to bury her in the cemetery for the Dominicans, but the townspeople wanted her buried in the church. A big argument broke out right there in the church. Someone at the funeral brought their disabled daughter and laid her down next to the body of Margaret. People saw Margaret's hand move and touch the girl, and immediately the girl was cured. Everyone rejoiced, and they now had miraculous proof that Margaret should be considered a saint.

The people got their wish, and Margaret was buried in the Dominican church. Thousands of people go to the Dominican church in Castello, Italy, every year to visit her and ask for her help.

PRAYER

*Blessed Margaret, you are such a good example
to me! I want to be like you and totally trust
God. Pray for me and help me never forget that
God made me who I am, loves me exactly
as I am, and will take care of me no matter
what happens in my life. Pray for me when
I feel left out or unloved, since you know how
that feels. Help me see my disability as a way
to serve and love God. Amen.*

SAINT SERVULUS

Patron of People
with Cerebral Palsy

P EOPLE OFTEN THINK SAINTS ACCOMPLISH AMAZ-
ING THINGS FOR GOD. Some saints are great
teachers and help many people come to know
God. Others take care of the sick and dying and
perform many acts of mercy. Others go live away from the
world and devote themselves entirely to prayer. St. Servulus
didn't do any of these things. In fact, he couldn't really do
anything by himself. He couldn't walk or even sit up by
himself. He needed help eating and rolling over on the
mat he laid on. This was because Servulus was born with
cerebral palsy. His muscles were very tight, and it was hard
for him to move. His mother and brother took care of
Servulus his whole life. His family was very poor, but they
did their best to help Servulus. Servulus also did what he
could to help his family.

St. Servulus lived in Rome way back in the 500s. At that
time, and even in some parts of the world today, people
with disabilities couldn't go to school, get jobs, or do many
other things most people take for granted. Servulus even
lived before wheelchairs existed. When he was old enough,
his mother and brother would carry him on his mat to the
front of Saint Clement Church, where he would sit and beg
for money. This was a common way for people who were
poor and disabled to earn a living in those days. Everyone in
the city got to know him since he was always there begging.
He was there day after day in all kinds of weather, lying on
his mat asking passersby to show him some kindness and
give him anything they could afford to spare.

Servulus would not only ask for alms, but he would also ask people who were coming and going from the church to stop and read passages of the Bible to him. He was very smart and could memorize the passages just by listening to them. He thought about the Scriptures all the time. He spent his days and even part of his nights reciting gospel passages and singing psalms he had memorized.

Servulus especially liked to think about the Passion of Jesus, and he united his own pain and suffering to Jesus. He never complained or was upset that he wasn't like other people. Instead of being frustrated that he was so dependent on others to take care of him and provide for his family, he actually was constantly giving thanks to God that he was able to share a little in the sufferings of Jesus. He knew Jesus grew up in a poor family too. He knew Jesus went through a lot of physical pain and mental suffering during his Passion. Servulus, too, had pain from his tight muscles, and he sometimes was insulted by people as they walked by him on the street.

Many people gave alms to Servulus. Maybe some felt sorry for him, but others were impressed and inspired by his example. So many people gave him money that it was said he grew rich in his poverty. Servulus only kept enough money for himself and his family to get by on. He shared the rest with other poor people who were always hanging around him, learning from his words and example. Everyone could see what a cheerful, generous person he was, and they wanted to be his friend. In this way, Servulus shared Jesus with others.

We don't know for sure how many years he lived, but we know that all of his friends, including those whom he shared with, were with him as he was dying. They were praying and singing hymns, when all of a sudden Servulus cried out, "Silence; do you not hear the sweet melody and praises which resound in the heavens?" The man who loved to praise God by singing was able to hear the angels in heaven singing.

Servulus died not long after this, in the year 590. He was buried in St. Clement Church, and many favors and miracles have happened for those who ask him for help. His feast day is December 23.

We know about Servulus because St. Gregory the Great knew him and talked about him in a homily. Gregory held up Servulus as an example of what it means to truly be holy.

PRAYER

Saint Servulus, help me follow your example. May I always thank God for my family and friends, and for all the help they give me. Always remind me that to God, loving him and loving others are a lot more important than achieving great things. I hope that by being a good friend to others we all grow closer to Jesus. Help me find ways to make a difference in their lives and let them know what a difference they make in mine. And help me to thank Jesus for making me the person I am. Amen.

BLESSED HERMAN

*Patron of People
with Spina Bifida, Cerebral Palsy,
or Cleft Palate*

I N 1013 A NOBLE FAMILY HAD A SON NAMED HERMAN. Herman wasn't like other little boys, and he couldn't do things that most other children were able to do. He couldn't walk or sit up by himself, and when he talked, it was almost impossible for anyone to understand him. There were many things wrong with Herman. The doctors thought he would only live a few years, but he lived for forty years and accomplished some incredible things.

Herman had several disabilities. He was born with a cleft palate, so it was hard to understand his speech. Today there are medical ways to help a person born with a cleft palate, but nothing like that was available when Herman lived. Herman also had cerebral palsy, which probably made it very hard for people to figure out what he was saying. It also made it hard for him to control his muscles and make them do what they were supposed to do. Plus, he had spina bifida, which basically affected the lower half of his body and prevented it from working properly.

God did bless Herman in other ways. Herman had a very strong will. Once he decided he wanted to do something, he didn't let his disabilities stop him. He was also very intelligent.

Herman lived with his family until he was about seven years old. Then his parents sent him to live with Benedictine monks on Reichenau Island in a place in southern Germany called Lake Constance. This turned out to be a very good thing for him. The monks took good care of him and loved him very much. They all enjoyed this enthusiastic, curious boy. When Herman was twenty he joined their community and became a monk too.

The monks gave Herman an excellent education, and Herman learned far more than most people—and probably much more than anyone thought would be possible for him. He had to work much harder than other children to force his body to cooperate, just so he could read and write. Everything was more difficult and took more concentration for him, but all his efforts and hard work would pay off. Herman became an expert in many subjects, including history, theology, math, astronomy, and music. He also learned several languages, including Arabic, Greek, and Latin. His achievements in these areas were amazing.

Herman was such an expert in history that he compiled the most complete list of important events in history from the birth of Jesus up to his own time. Obviously, it would take a lot of patience for anyone to do all the research to make an accurate detailed list. It must have taken even more patience and hard work for Herman to do all the reading and writing that was necessary to see this project through. It probably took years, but giving up was just not his style.

As if that wasn't enough to keep him busy, he made musical instruments and even invented new gadgets to help him study the stars. It must have been hard for him to build these things. He couldn't stand or even sit up by himself.

When he wasn't sitting with some help, he probably did most things from his bed or from a mat he would lie on. His determination forced his body to accomplish what he set his mind on.

He loved poetry too. He is considered the most famous poet of his time. Toward the end of his life Herman lost his sight, but even that didn't stop him. He continued to compose poems and hymns. People have long thought that he wrote the Hail, Holy Queen (Salve Regina), which everyone still prays today at the end of the Rosary. He also wrote another famous hymn to Our Lady called *Alma Redemptoris Mater* that is still sung in churches. He definitely wasn't a singer. He could barely speak. It was his love for God and Our Lady that led him to write these beautiful hymns.

Many people came from all over to learn and study under Herman. Of course they had heard how intelligent he was, but they also heard how holy he was, and they wanted to learn from his example. Plus, Herman had a great personality and was a joy to be with. This, too, was because he loved God so much.

Herman died in the year 1054. He probably lived his whole life in the monastery and likely didn't know very many people. But all his achievements and contributions to so many areas made him well known. People called him Herman the Cripple or Herman the Lame. They weren't trying to be mean or disrespectful. At the time it was just the common way to refer to someone with a disability. Maybe it was a good thing, because people came to understand that even if someone had a disability, with God's help and their own determination, almost anything was possible. It was also common to refer to people by where they were from, so even today he is known as Herman Contractus or Herman of Reichenau.

Long after his death, people still remembered him for his holiness. They started praying to him to help them. They passed this devotion down from generation to generation for eight hundred years, and in 1863 Herman was beatified by Pope Pius IX. His feast day is September 25.

PRAYER

Blessed Herman, please pray for me.
Ask God to give me the grace never to give up
even if it's harder and takes me longer to do
things. Help me to know that even though my
body might not do what I want, with God's
help, I can accomplish anything I set my mind
to. Help me to have a special love for Our Lady
and honor her as you did. Amen.

Special Saints for Special People

Hail, holy Queen,

Mother of mercy, our life,
our sweetness and our hope.
To thee do we cry, poor banished children of Eve.
To thee do we send up our sighs, mourning
and weeping in this valley of tears.
Turn, then, most gracious advocate,
thine eyes of mercy toward us, and after this,
our exile, show unto us the blessed fruit
of thy womb, Jesus. O clement, O loving,
O sweet Virgin Mary.
Pray for us, O holy Mother of God.
That we may be made worthy
of the promises of Christ.
Amen.

SAINT JOSEPH OF CUPERTINO

*Patron of People
with Developmental
Disabilities*

IT'S ONE THING TO BE SMART. It's another thing to be holy. It's one thing to be seen as normal, but how God sees a person and how other people see the same person can be two very different things.

In the early 1600s Joseph of Cupertino was born in a small town in southeast Italy. There wasn't one person in his whole life who thought of him as just another person like everybody else. Everyone who knew him thought he was weird.

Even Joseph knew he was different. His whole life he was forgetful and absentminded. He would start to do something but not finish. Or he would start to tell a story, but then suddenly his thoughts would wander off and he wouldn't even remember that he was talking. He was so forgetful that sometimes he wouldn't even remember to eat. And when he was reminded, he'd just say, "I forgot." He would wander around with his mouth hanging open, not going anywhere in particular.

No matter how hard Joseph tried, he just didn't seem to fit in. Sudden noises made him jump and drop whatever he had in his hands. People would laugh at him because he was so different from anyone else they knew. Even if people tried to be nice to him, they found it almost impossible.

Joseph's parents had a hard life. They were very poor. Joseph was born in the shed behind their house because the house was being taken away from them and everything they owned was being sold just to pay the bills.

Joseph usually didn't have enough to eat as a child and was sick quite often. This alone made it hard on his parents, but all of his odd behavior made things even worse. His mother would punish him severely, trying to correct his behavior, but it never helped. His teachers definitely didn't know what to do with him. He was not a very good student at all. Other children would try to play with him, but he always seemed to start daydreaming and to be in his own world. When he was old enough to work, he took a job with a shoemaker, but Joseph wasn't very good at it. The shoemaker felt sorry for him and put up with all of his odd behavior but found him to be more trouble than not. Joseph just couldn't learn the skills needed for the job. Again, Joseph knew this job really didn't suit him and knew his life was going nowhere fast.

One day, while he was at work he saw a friar come into town begging for food, and an idea popped into Joseph's head. He could become a Franciscan friar. After all, he knew he didn't have to be educated or reliable to beg for food. And he had two uncles who were Franciscans, so that gave him encouragement too. His parents were only too happy to let him go find a community that would accept him. There would be one less mouth to feed at home, and they wouldn't have to put up with him anymore and be embarrassed by his behavior. A son who was part of a religious community was something they could be proud of.

So Joseph went off searching for a community to accept him, but time after time he was rejected. The fact that he had no education and that there was obviously something different about him made it seem almost impossible for any community to accept him. Joseph didn't argue with them, because he knew they were right in rejecting him. Finally, one community agreed to take him on a trial basis but only as a lay brother, not as a full member of their community.

Unfortunately, things didn't work out here for Joseph either. The members of the community tried to be nice to him, but time after time, no matter how hard Joseph tried, he just couldn't do anything right. He was impossible to teach. And they weren't able to accept his behavior any better than anyone else ever had. He would be washing dishes and all of a sudden fall to his knees and start praying, becoming totally unaware of everything around him. Or he would be carrying plates filled with everyone's food, and for no reason at all, suddenly forget what he was doing and let everything crash to the floor. They even made him wear pieces of the broken plates on his robe to remind him not to let himself become so distracted again, but even that didn't help.

In the end, the community forced Joseph to leave them. He never forgot that day and said it was the worst day of his life. He made his way back to his parents' house, but they weren't pleased to welcome him home. His mother was upset that he got himself thrown out. She was angry that he had returned home and would again become her responsibility. She was embarrassed about what her neighbors would say. And she was also very angry about how the community treated her son.

Since her brother was a member of the community and held a high office, she went to give him a piece of her mind. She begged him to make the community take Joseph back, just so she could be rid of him. She didn't care what happened to him or what would become of him, as long as he wasn't her responsibility. The best her brother could agree to was to accept Joseph back as a servant for the community and as a worker out in the stable where he couldn't do much harm.

Joseph accepted this. Something inside Joseph began to change. He assumed this was all he could expect in life and was grateful to at least have a job. Never complaining, Joseph happily accepted whatever food and clothes they provided for him, slept on a plank in the barn, and cheerfully did any task that they asked of him. He actually liked living with the animals and enjoyed the smallest pleasures that came his way. The other friars would go down to the barn from time to time and began to see how joyous he was. He was always eager to help them and never showed any care for himself. He would go out begging on their behalf in his free time even though he wasn't required to. The other friars began to notice that the poorest people of the city were the most accepting of Joseph. They were able to look beyond his behavior and see the kind-hearted, joyful man Joseph was.

After a lot of debate among the friars, it was decided to

accept Joseph back into the community. They decided to try to give him enough of an education so that he could become a priest. This seemed impossible. They tried their best, and Joseph tried his best, too, but he could barely learn to read and write. When they had him practice giving homilies, the only verse out of the whole Bible that he could speak about was the part in Luke's gospel when a woman in the crowd called out to Jesus, "Blessed is the womb that carried you and the breasts at which you nursed."

To become a priest, Joseph would have to pass two tests given by the bishop. The first test would make him a deacon, and a year later a second test would allow him to be ordained a priest. No one thought he had a chance of passing either test. When the day came for the first exam, a nervous Joseph waited to meet with the bishop. When Joseph's turn came, the bishop randomly opened his Bible and asked Joseph to explain the verse he read. The bishop happened to read the very verse Joseph could easily talk about. Joseph went on and on making great points about this verse, and the bishop was very impressed. Joseph passed easily, and everyone in his community was amazed.

After another year of studying with little results Joseph again went to meet the bishop. Many other young men were also there for the exam, so Joseph had to wait his turn. The bishop was so impressed with the people who went before Joseph that he ended the whole exam, and everyone there, including Joseph, automatically passed and was ordained to the priesthood.

Joseph didn't think any more of himself just because he was a priest now. He knew what his abilities and limits were. He would still happily do the chores the other friars didn't want to do. He would do the dishes, sweep the floors, and quietly go about taking care of other duties that some people said priests shouldn't have to worry about. People who were poor continued to love and respect him for who he was. They liked having a priest who was simple and unselfish. Sometimes when Joseph returned to the monastery after being with poor people, the other friars would notice Joseph would be missing something—a sandal, or rosary, or part of his habit. His friends in town would want something to remind them of him. Joseph was as absentminded as ever and wouldn't even realize he was giving everything away. This would frustrate his superiors, even though he would return with his sack full of food because the poor were so generous with him.

Joseph was still forgetful and easily distracted, but people were beginning to understand how holy he was. He was still a pain to many people who were very practical and level-minded, but other people came to know that he was deep in prayer. It wasn't that he was daydreaming, but the slightest thing would make him marvel at how awesome it was that God created it, and he was able to see that God was reflected in it.

Occasionally, people will marvel at a beautiful sunset or a tall mountain, but Joseph would marvel over things most people don't even notice. He would be so deep in his thoughts that he would be totally unaware of everything around him. His brother friars would try to stick him with pins and even burn him with hot coals to snap him out of it, but Joseph never felt a thing. When he was lost in thought, he would be as still as a statue and completely unmovable. He had always been like this, but now he could be lost in thought for a whole day. Some people were beginning to understand that this was actually a special gift from God and not a defect in him, as most people had always assumed.

People who were around him during these times started noticing something else that was even more incredible. While Joseph was in these ecstasies, he would be lifted up off the ground and wouldn't even know it. They would see him floating in the air in whatever position he had been in on the ground. He could be kneeling in church or eating a meal. It didn't matter. When he got lost in his thoughts and prayers, he'd be lifted into the air.

Joseph began having other unexplainable powers too. Joseph was a Franciscan, and much like St. Francis of Assisi, Joseph always loved animals. About the same time as he started "flying," people started noticing that he could really communicate with the animals and they would obey him. There are many stories from people who witnessed his special gifts. There's a story about how once during harvest time all the people in the village were so busy they completely forgot to go to the prayer service they usually attended. Joseph wasn't very happy to find the chapel empty when he got there. There were sheep grazing in the nearby fields, so Joseph went out and called them into the chapel. The sheep obeyed without hesitation and came to the church. Joseph began the prayers and at the right times all of the sheep would reply "Baa." At the end he blessed them, and they all went back to the field as if nothing happened.

There was another story of how Joseph sent a small bird to the choir of a convent nearby. The bird would know when the sisters would sing and always come at the right times and sing along with them. Once a sister shooed the bird away and it didn't come back. Joseph knew what happened without anyone telling him. He promised the bird would return, and it did. Another time when it was Holy Week the sisters tied a small bell to the bird and again it didn't return. Joseph explained that bells aren't rung during Holy Week. Sure enough, the bird returned at Easter.

There were also many stories that sick and disabled people were being cured by Joseph. Everyone was talking of these wonderful and amazing miracles. Lots of people, especially among the poor, believed Joseph was a saint. There were, however, those who didn't believe that at all. After all, this was Joseph. He was the one who caused so much trouble. If God was going to give someone such amazing gifts, they'd say, then obviously he would give them to someone other than Joseph. These people thought Joseph was faking everything and reported him to superiors. Joseph was questioned and put on trial. At one point, even the pope questioned Joseph. No one could ever say he was guilty of anything, but they also didn't admit that these supernatural gifts were definitely from God.

Without really knowing what to do with him, they decided it would be best to make Joseph live in a remote place where he would only have contact with a few friars who were in charge of keeping close watch over him. He wasn't allowed to ever leave, and he couldn't even write letters to anyone. He felt like he was in jail, but he accepted this new trial and never questioned his superiors. All of his old friends among the poor kept finding out where he was, so poor Joseph was forced to move from place to place for the rest of his life. Even though he was cut off from the world, all of his experiences continued. Joseph knew things that were happening in the outside world without being told. He even knew that the pope had died before the news reached the other Franciscans.

In 1663, Joseph knew his time on earth was coming to an end. He was moved to yet another hiding place where he predicted that he would die. He even announced his death would occur on the first day that he didn't receive Holy Communion, and that was exactly how it happened. He became sick with a fever in August, but continued to say Mass every morning, or at least receive Holy Communion every day until September 18. Just as he predicted, he died that very same day, and now we celebrate his feast on that date every year.

PRAYER

Saint Joseph of Cupertino, you know what it feels like to be different. You know that sometimes people judge based on outward appearances, and not what is in our hearts. Help me to know that God understands me better than I even understand myself. He sees what is in my heart and doesn't judge me based on how successful or popular I am. Pray for me and help me to love God and everyone I know, since this is all that matters to God. Amen.

SAINT RENÉ GOUPIL

Patron of People with
Hearing Impairments

SAINT RENÉ GOUPIL WAS BORN IN FRANCE IN THE EARLY 1600s. He became a surgeon, but when he was in his thirties he felt called to enter the Jesuit order. Unfortunately, René only lasted for the first few months of the first year of training. He had to leave the seminary because he was almost totally deaf. There's no evidence René was born deaf. It seems likely that his deafness was from an illness he had shortly after entering the seminary.

René must have been very disappointed. Many Jesuits are missionaries who travel to other countries to spread the faith to people who don't know anything about Jesus. René really felt God was calling him to do that, too, so even though he couldn't be a Jesuit himself, he decided to volunteer to go to Canada with the Jesuits as a surgeon. Quebec at the time was a French settlement in Canada known as New France. It was hard for the missionaries and settlers to communicate with the native people, because the native people didn't speak French and the settlers and missionaries didn't know the native languages. We don't know if it was even harder for René to communicate with the native people. On one hand, it was useless to try to read their lips since he didn't speak their language. On the other hand, he was probably better at reading their faces and body language than the other missionaries, since he was already used to doing this when communicating with anyone.

For the next couple years, he worked in a hospital in Quebec with local villagers. Even though René was doing a lot of important work and knew that he was using the talents God gave him, he continued to wish he could do more to spread the faith in this new land. He tried to see Jesus in each patient he treated. At the same time, René followed all the directions of the Jesuit superiors. He lived in their house, and they had him do the most basic chores. René accepted the work, even though he wasn't required to obey them since he was not a Jesuit. All of this helped him grow in humility and love for others.

René volunteered to go on a dangerous mission with Father Isaac Jogues, who was returning with a group of about forty other Jesuits and Huron Indians to Huronia, the name the French gave to the main terriroty of the Hurons. Father Jogues happily accepted René because he knew a surgeon would be needed at the Huronia mission. As the canoes made their way up the St. Lawrence River, they were attacked and captured by a large group of Iroquois Indians, who were at war with the Hurons and their French friends. Almost all of the Hurons they were traveling with fled and were able to escape, but the missionaries were not so fortunate. They were brutally treated by the Iroquois and tortured in many ways.

As prisoners, they continued to travel on the river in their canoes. René told Fr. Isaac Jogues of his desire to be a Jesuit, and knowing the possible dangers that were ahead, Fr. Jogues let him make his profession right there in the canoe. René finally obtained his wish to become a Jesuit.

As they continued to travel, Father Jogues witnessed many

of René's amazing virtues. René, who was badly injured himself, did his best to help others who were injured during the fight. Not only did he care for other prisoners, but he also did everything possible to help the injured Iroquois who had captured them and treated them so cruelly. He also didn't resist, as Father Jogues did, when the Iroquois forced him to help paddle the canoe. There were also some opportunities for René to escape, and Father Jogues tried to convince him to save his life, but René wanted to leave everything up to God's will and was ready to be martyred. René was always praying as they traveled.

In village after village, the Iroquois tortured them relentlessly. René handled all these torments and kept praying.

Their captors took them to their village in what is now Auriesville, New York. There, René stayed in a cabin and often said his prayers in front of the Iroquois, which an old Iroquois man didn't like. René, who always loved children, was playing with some of the Iroquois children. He took a child's hand and guided it as he taught him how to make the Sign of the Cross. The old Iroquois mistakenly believed that Rene was putting a curse on the boy. He got very angry and ordered a younger Iroquois to kill René. The younger Iroquois went out and met René and Father Isaac Jogues as they were returning to the village after being allowed to go pray in the wilderness. The young Iroquois carried out his orders and killed René while Isaac Jogues and the others watched helplessly. The Iroquois didn't even allow René to be buried properly. First they threw his body in the river. Then after Father Jogues found it, the Iroquois secretly dragged it into the forest .

We know the story of René Goupil thanks to a letter that Father Isaac Jogues wrote to his Jesuit superiors in France a few years after René's death. Father Jogues praised him for his holy life serving God and dying as a martyr while trying to spread the faith.

Father Isaac Jogues and six other missionaries were also eventually martyred on different missionary trips. Today, we remember the eight North American Martyrs every October 19.

PRAYER

Saint René, thank you for your example.
You were prevented from entering the Jesuits
because of your disability, but you were faithful
and did what you could to serve God. Through
your prayers, help me to recognize and use the
talents that God has given me. Help me to have
the courage not to let my disability stop me from
doing what I think God wants me to do. Even if
things don't work out as easily for me as they do
for others, help me to have the courage always to
trust God and know that God's will for me will
be accomplished. Amen.

SAINT LIDWINA

*Patron of People
with Multiple Sclerosis*

N O ONE LIKES TO BE SICK. No one enjoys suffering. And when we do get sick we want to
know what is happening and how to treat it
so we can get better. When doctors can't help
and can't even explain what's wrong, it can be an even
greater burden. That's what happened in St. Lidwina's life.

Lidwina lived in a town called Schiedam in what is
now the Netherlands from 1380 to 1433. She was perfectly
healthy until she was about fifteen years old. She was
having fun ice skating with some of her friends when she
took a very bad fall and broke a rib. Most people recover
after an injury like that, but Lidwina didn't. In fact, she
got worse and worse for the rest of her life. She suffered
from all kinds of problems. For one thing, the wound
from the fall got infected. She developed sores all over her
body. She couldn't walk and eventually became paralyzed,
except for her left hand. She suffered from bad pain and
even had terrible pain in her teeth. She also ate little to
nothing and didn't sleep much. Eventually, she lost her
sight. Sometimes she would bleed and no one knew why.
As the months and years went by, her whole body was in
pain. From the time she fell until she died thirty-eight
years later, she was in bed, wracked with pain and totally
dependent on her family.

All these painful burdens would be enough to make
anyone question God and lose hope. In the beginning
it was no different for Lidwina. She had wanted to serve
God and didn't understand why these bad things were

happening to her. It took time and the help of a priest for her to realize that she was serving God by uniting all of these unexplainable sufferings to him. Instead of being resentful and upset that she was in so much pain all the time, she was grateful to God and saw it as a gift. Surely it wasn't what she had in mind when as a child she desired to devote herself to God, but she now realized that her life wasn't a waste. She was suffering in union with Jesus, who suffered so much on the cross.

Many people thought she was very holy and believed God was granting special favors to her. Reports began to spread of visions, miracles, and healings occurring at her bedside. She had visitors from the town as well as some famous people who traveled far just to see her. Some holy people wrote biographies about her, which still exist and help us to know about her life. Others just wanted her friendship and advice because they recognized that her suffering was drawing her close to God. Somehow God would reveal things to her and give her special knowledge.

As if all of her physical suffering wasn't enough, she knew that some people thought she was faking. Others thought she might be possessed by an evil spirit. She offered these trials to God too. Even the priest wasn't sure what to think, so one day he decided to test her. He brought her an unconsecrated host. Lidwina knew right away that it was not the Body of Christ, which helped prove her holiness to the priest.

In one of her many visions she saw a rose bush, and

God told her that her suffering would end when she saw the bush in bloom. She did see it come true in another vision shortly before she died on Easter morning, April 14, 1433. Just before she died she also saw Jesus coming to her to give her the last sacrament.

Almost immediately after her death, people started going to her grave praying to her for favors. Through the years they never stopped asking for her intercession. She wasn't officially declared a saint until March 14, 1890, by Pope Leo XIII. We remember her on her feast day every April 14.

Scientists and doctors recently have studied everything written about her as well as the skeletal remains that still exist and are venerated as relics. While it's impossible to know for certain, they believe Lidwina probably had multiple sclerosis or MS. Multiple sclerosis usually strikes at around the age Lidwina became ill, and her symptoms were very similar to the symptoms of MS. Even the long duration of Lidwina's suffering and the slow, continuous decline of her health are consistent with MS. If Lidwina did have MS, as many people believe, she would be the earliest person we know of to have suffered from this illness.

Lidwina is the patron of ice skaters and the chronically ill. Many people with MS ask for her help as well. Even if she didn't have MS, she certainly understands the trials that people with MS experience. She also understands the trials of anyone who is seeking answers to unexplainable medical conditions. Sometimes not knowing what is wrong and having to just trust God is the hardest part. Lidwina is a good example for everyone.

PRAYER

Saint Lidwina, pray for me, especially in times of pain and uncertainty. Through your prayers help me to know that God can take my pain and use it in ways I might not even understand. Even though it may look to others like my life is not very useful, help me learn to trust God, even if things are likely to get worse. May I truly know that my suffering is used by God for good. Finally, please pray for me in those times when answers aren't readily available. Help me also to offer God the pain that comes from not having answers. Amen.

SAINT PAULINA

Patron of People
with Diabetes

A MABILE LUCIA VISINTAINER WAS BORN ON DECEMBER 16, 1865, IN WHAT IS NOW TRENT, ITALY. Today we know her as St. Paulina, and she was the first saint to be canonized from Brazil.

As a small child she worked at a silk mill in her hometown just to try to help her family earn money to live on. They and many of their neighbors were very poor. When Amabile was only ten years old, her family moved to Brazil to try to make a better life for themselves. About fifty of their own friends and neighbors were with them as their ship sailed across the Atlantic Ocean. When they arrived in Brazil, they settled in the state of St. Catherine and set up a village called Vigolo, which is now known as Nova Trento.

Amabile was twelve years old when she made her First Communion, and although she didn't have much of an education, she was very interested in the Catholic faith. She did her best to learn everything she could and tried to practice everything she learned. As a teenager she would help clean the church, visit the sick, and teach children in her parish. She also had a lot of responsibilities at home with all of her brothers and sisters. Her mother died in 1886 while giving birth to her thirteenth child. So at the age of twenty-one, Amabile was responsible for raising her siblings until her father remarried.

In 1890 Amabile and her friend Virginia were taking care of a woman with cancer. From this experience, they and a third friend, named Teresa, decided to start a new religious order. They received the approval of their bishop, and their new order became known as the Congregation of the Little Sisters of the Immaculate Conception. From then on Amabile became known as Sister Paulina of the Agonizing Heart of Jesus. She was twenty-five years old. There were other religious orders in the country at this time, but theirs was the first to be started within Brazil.

The order grew very quickly, and within three years Sister Paulina was elected head of the order as Mother Superior General. She left her local town to go to a different city to take care of the unwanted. She helped look after orphans, children of slaves, and older slaves who were left to die when they were no longer able to work.

Sr. Paulina was supposed to hold this position as Superior General for the rest of her life, but within six years there were disagreements about her leadership. She had to step down from being Superior General and wasn't allowed any active role in the congregation she started. She was sent to another city to work with the elderly and sick in Saint Vincent De Paul Hospital. (Saint Vincent de Paul is another famous saint known for helping people in need, and even today many hospitals and organizations are named after him.)

Paulina stayed there for fifteen years. She was not upset or bitter about the way she was treated by her own order. In fact, all of Paulina's free time was spent praying for the congregation and its work and success. Finally she was called back to the congregation in 1918. From then on Sr. Paulina lived a cloistered life in the convent, praying and taking care of sick sisters. In May of 1933, the pope formally recognized Sr. Paulina as Venerable Mother Foundress.

Throughout almost her whole life Mother Paulina had diabetes. People back then didn't have the ways to test and control blood sugar that we have today. Sr. Paulina likely worked hard watching what she ate. Even though she always was responsible for others, she also needed to always be concerned for her own health. She had to make sure she stayed healthy so she could help others. Whether she was taking care of her family or assisting others as she grew older, Mother Paulina knew that she was no good to others unless she looked after herself too. She didn't let diabetes stop her from doing what she knew God was calling her to do, but watching what she ate and the effects different foods had on her was a constant concern. Traveling and possibly even immigrating to the new country was probably a little harder for her too. She couldn't easily eat anything that was offered, and she couldn't just skip meals when traveling.

God often uses our own experiences and trials to shape how we look at others. Her own health probably helped her to be more compassionate. She knew how to show charity, and she probably had first-hand experience of others showing her charity at times when she felt weak and needed something to eat.

The effects of diabetes can be hard. During the last four years of her life, diabetes brought many crosses to

Mother Paulina. In 1938 she started going blind from the disease, which is a common risk factor. She also had an infection from a small cut on her finger, and the finger had to be removed. Unfortunately, this didn't get rid of the infection, and she had to have more operations, removing first her hand and then her arm. She also developed lung cancer, and the cancer and the infection led to her death on July 9, 1942.

In 1981 Pope John Paul II beatified Paulina, and he declared her a saint in 2002. Some of St. Paulina's relatives run a center dedicated to her in Kulpmont, Pennsylvania, where they display one of her relics for visitors to see.

We celebrate her feast day on July 9.

PRAYER

*Saint Paulina, help me to be as
generous a person as you were. Like you,
I need to take care of myself, but through your
prayers, teach me how to go on with my life
and how to help others. Help me to know that
my experiences shape how I treat others, and
therefore I should try to be grateful for the
person God made me to be. Amen.*

SAINT BERNADETTE SOUBIROUS

Patron of People
with Asthma

M ANY PEOPLE HAVE HEARD THE STORY OF OUR LADY APPEARING IN LOURDES, FRANCE, IN 1858 TO A YOUNG GIRL NAMED BERNADETTE SOUBIROUS. It is well known that Mary, calling herself the Immaculate Conception, appeared to Bernadette many times, asking for people to pray, do penance, and build a chapel in her honor. Everyone also knows about the spring of water that sprang up from the muddy soil that Mary asked Bernadette to wash and drink from as an act of penance. Today, Lourdes is one of the most popular shrines for Catholics to visit.

What some people are surprised to know is that Bernadette had severe asthma her whole life. She was born January 7, 1844. Her father, Francis, was a flour miller, and her mother, Louise, did laundry for wealthy people in the town. Bernadette was the oldest of five children. (She had other brothers and sisters who didn't live very long after birth.) The Soubirous family was a happy, holy family that loved each other and their Catholic faith very much.

Bernadette was often sick as a child and developed asthma when she was about six years old. She would lose her breath easily, she would begin coughing and wheezing, and her chest would tighten up. Her parents were always worried about her. They were so concerned that when she was thirteen she was sent to a mountain area to live with a family who had taken care of her as a baby. Her parents hoped that the fresh air would help her.

Bernadette tried to fit in with this foster family, doing

any chore they asked of her, including watching the family's sheep each day as they grazed in the mountains. But Bernadette was lonely and missed her family very much. She returned to Lourdes after a year or so.

Many families in Lourdes went through hard times in the 1850s, and the Soubirous family was no different. They had always been poor, but things got even harder for them, and they were forced to move into a very small room in the former town jail. It was such an awful place that it was nicknamed the Dungeon. These conditions weren't very helpful in preventing Bernadette's asthma attacks, but the family did their best to help her.

Despite this hardship, this was a happy time for Bernadette. Not only was she back home with her family, she also began school with the Sisters of Charity and Christian Instruction, whose motherhouse is in Nevers, in central France. Bernadette would have been shocked if anyone told her that someday she would join the order. She was just so overjoyed to be getting an education, especially religious instruction so she could finally receive her First Communion. She had desired this for a long time. Her foster mother had tried to teach her some basic lessons of the faith but quickly gave up, because she didn't think Bernadette was smart enough to learn. Most people thought of Bernadette as a quiet, shy, uneducated girl who was a hard worker but would never be anyone special. But the nuns and her new classmates soon got to know the real Bernadette. She was a joyful person with a great sense of humor who liked to laugh and joke with her friends. Everyone loved to be with her.

On that famous day of February 11, 1858, when Our Lady first appeared to Bernadette in the grotto, her mother hesitated to let Bernadette, who had just come home from school, go out with her sister and a friend to collect firewood. After being allowed to go, Bernadette was careful to take precautions not to get sick and cause her asthma to act up. She didn't carelessly cross a stream of icy, cold water as the other girls did even though it was freezing that day. She first looked for a dry area for crossing to the other side where firewood could be gathered. When she wasn't able to find one, she stopped to remove her shoes and stockings before walking through the stream. She knew walking around with wet feet would cause her asthma to be worse. This gave her friends a head start as Bernadette struggled to catch up with them, but it was this separation that Our Lady chose to use to appear only to Bernadette.

At first, most people didn't believe Bernadette. Everyone thought she was making up the story of seeing "a beautiful lady" who wore a long white veil with a blue sash around her waist and a golden rose on each foot. Her parents didn't believe her and didn't want Bernadette to return to the grotto anymore, even though Bernadette had wanted to go back very badly. They relented, though, and eventually came to believe their daughter. Bernadette returned to the grotto and had a total of eighteen visions over the next few months. The priest doubted that the Virgin Mary would appear to such a poor, uneducated girl to ask that a chapel be built. The sisters who taught her in school strictly forbade all of the girls from thinking and talking about it. The civil authorities went to great lengths questioning Bernadette for hours, threatening her, and trying to force her to change her story. All of these trials caused more asthma attacks, weakening Bernadette. As news of the visions spread, the townspeople and pilgrims from near and far also peppered Bernadette with many requests and favors. They also tried to win the family's help by bringing them gifts. Bernadette always insisted that none of the gifts be accepted even though they would have helped her family. She and her family were under a lot of stress, which was not helpful for preventing the asthma from flaring up.

In one vision, the beautiful lady had Bernadette dig in some dirt in the grotto. Bernadette soon found a trickle of water and was then told to wash her face and drink from the newly discovered muddy spring. By the next day, that little dirty pool of water had turned into the clean, clear, cool flowing stream that we know today.

Quickly there began to be reports that the water from this new spring had special powers to heal. Unexplainable healings and cures began happening almost immediately. In her heart, however, Bernadette knew and readily accepted that the water was not meant to heal her from her asthma attacks. This is contrary to the way most of us would think. After all, since Our Lady appeared to her, and since she had gone through so much trouble convincing her family, the town, and the church that the apparitions were real, surely our most loving Mother would cure her. Bernadette never asked for this, because she knew it was a way she could do the penance that Our Lady asked for. Our Lady had told her that she would not be happy in this world, only in the next, and Bernadette accepted this fate without complaint.

Bernadette would eventually go to live with the Sisters of Nevers to try to escape her new fame. First, she lived at the convent in Lourdes, and later when she had decided to become a nun herself, she moved to Nevers. Bernadette's life didn't become any easier in the convent. There were still some who didn't believe her, but a great many others did and wanted her to repeat the story over and over again, which Bernadette patiently did since she thought it might help others grow closer to God. Her superiors in the convent also made life hard for Bernadette. They thought her popularity would have a bad effect on her and make her proud and arrogant, so they gave Bernadette many hard tasks and humiliating penances. It took years for them to realize Bernadette was a special person.

Bernadette's health in the convent only grew worse. On top of asthma, she developed tuberculosis and was often in the infirmary. When her health permitted, she had duties in the kitchen, infirmary, or chapel doing the needlepoint for the priests' vestments. She always did all her work cheerfully and without complaint, no matter how she felt.

Bernadette died on April 16, 1879, saying, "Blessed Mary, Mother of God, pray for me! A poor sinner, a poor sinner." April 16 is now her feast day. Many people also associate her with February 11, the Feast of Our Lady of Lourdes. December 8, 1933 was the date of her canonization, which was quite fitting since that's the Solemnity of the Immaculate Conception, which was popularized by the apparitions to Bernadette at Lourdes.

PRAYER

*Saint Bernadette, you were favored with visits
from our heavenly Mother and yet your life
was not easy. You struggled with asthma and
other illnesses, not to mention poverty and
loneliness. You realized that God doesn't always
make this life easy for us, even though he loves
us. Mary told you that you would be happy in
heaven, but not here on earth, and yet you were
a cheerful, giving person. Help me to accept the
trials God gives me without complaining.
And help me to be devoted to Our Lady,
knowing that she will take care of me. Amen.*

SAINT KATERI TEKAKWITHA

*Patron of People
with Facial Deformities
or Visual Impairments*

O N October 21, 2012, Native Americans rejoiced as Pope Benedict XVI declared Kateri Tekakwitha a saint. As well as being the first Native American saint, Kateri is usually thought of as the patron of those who love nature and work to preserve the environment. People don't always know that she was disabled.

Kateri Tekakwitha was born in 1656 in a village near what is now Auriesville, New York. Her father was a Mohawk chief and her mother was an Algonquin Indian. Her mother was also a Catholic convert. When Kateri was only four years old, smallpox broke out and many people in her tribe died, including Kateri's parents and baby brother. Kateri was very sick, too, but survived. She recovered from the illness itself, but it left ugly scars all over her body and face. Her eyes were also very badly damaged, and she was visually impaired. The sunlight really bothered her eyes and made it almost impossible for her to see. She would usually have to feel her way around. In fact, people nicknamed her Tekakwitha, which meant "she who bumps into things."

After the plague, the people moved about five miles away and set up a new village in what is now Fonda, New York. Two aunts and an uncle, who was also a chief, adopted Kateri. She was quiet and shy with a sweet personality, and she spent her childhood in the same way as other Native American children. Her days were filled with chores, helping her aunts with the crops they grew, searching in the woods for roots they used to make medicine and dye, and helping them take care of their home. Even though her eyesight was very poor, Kateri also became quite good at beadwork. Like all the other children, Kateri's future was being planned for from a very young age. When she was only eight years old, the elders decided who she was supposed to marry when she grew up.

When Kateri was eighteen, some Jesuit missionaries came to the village. Kateri could vaguely remember how her mother would pray and talk about God. She was very interested in learning from these strangers. Although she wasn't a Christian, she would often like to be alone with God to pray and be with him in nature. Her uncle, on the other hand, did not like anything about these "black robes." He didn't trust them because previous settlers had mistreated the Native Americans and brought diseases, like the smallpox epidemic that killed Kateri's family and so many others. Only very reluctantly did he allow Kateri to learn about Christianity.

When Kateri was twenty she was baptized a Catholic on Easter Sunday 1676. She was thrilled, but the rest of her family and village did not agree with her decision. Kateri's life became very hard. Everyone treated her like an outcast. Christians believe Sundays are a day of rest. Therefore, every Sunday Kateri was denied food since she would not work alongside everyone else. They threatened to torture or even kill her if she didn't give up this new religion, but Kateri remained faithful. As the months went by, her life became harder and harder, and yet Kateri's desire to devote her life totally to God only continued to grow.

Kateri realized that she needed to leave her village for her own safety. The missionaries recommended she go to Saint Francis Xavier du Sault mission near Montreal, Canada. So one night she started a two-hundred mile trip to her new home. This meant traveling unfamiliar woods, rivers, and swamps. This would be dangerous for anyone, but especially for the girl who bumped into things. It took her two months.

The Christians in the new village were amazed she survived the journey but quickly came to see her determination in the way she dedicated herself to God. The priests in the mission were so impressed with her that she was allowed to make her First Communion just a few months later on Christmas Day 1677.

The next year, Kateri took a vow to dedicate the rest of her life totally to God and never marry. She was the first Native American known to do this. Kateri hoped to start a convent of Native American sisters, but because of her poor health, the priests discouraged her. She humbly accepted their advice.

Kateri wasn't educated and couldn't read and write, but people would often ask her to tell them a story. She was able to remember everything she had learned about Jesus, and she gladly shared it with others. The way she lived her life as a Christian was also an inspiration. Her motto in life became, "Who can tell me what is most pleasing to God, that I may do it?" She helped the elderly and sick, took care of the children, and had a kind word for everyone she talked to. Her prayer life was intense. She loved the Rosary and always wore one around her neck. She would make little crosses and place them around the woods like Stations of the Cross to remind her to stop and pray. She did lots of very hard penances asking God to convert others. In the winter when it was hunting season and most people were away, Kateri would be found kneeling in the snow praying. People would try to sit close to Kateri in church because they felt closer to God. Some people even said that sometimes her face would change and become peaceful and beautiful, like she was looking at God. (Remember that Kateri had many scars on her face from smallpox.) Kateri only lived for about three years in her new village. The hard life and the extreme penances she undertook took a toll on her health. When she died on April 17, 1680, people who were with her said the scars and lines from years of suffering immediately disappeared from her face. They said she became as beautiful and radiant as a child. She was not quite twenty-four years old. Today the church remembers Kateri every July 14. She is called the Lily of the Mohawks because she was so lovely and pure.

PRAYER

*Saint Kateri, you followed God
no matter what. You were quiet and shy,
but you didn't let other people run your life
or tell you what to believe. Pray for me.
Help me not to let my challenges stop me
from following God's will for me, and help
me to serve God in whatever way
he wants. Amen.*